Reviving the
Local Church

Reviving the Local Church

David J. Ernsberger

Fortress Press

Philadelphia, Pa.

Library of Congress Catalog Card Number 69–14624

825A69   Printed in U. S. A.   1–192

FOREWORD

It is a pleasure to initiate the Church-in-Mission Series with a presentation that is at once practical, functional, and theological. David Ernsberger's insights have been forged in the crucible of day-to-day experience as a parish pastor, not in an ivory tower. He has taught and learned from his congregation much about the meaning of witness, fellowship, service, and nurture as primary functions of the church. The fruit of that experience is here distilled within a theological framework centered in Christ and in a biblical conception of the church. Pastors, church officers and teachers, and all Christians concerned with fostering active discipleship will welcome the down-to-earth suggestions set forth in this volume.

Mr. Ernsberger is an acknowledged authority on Christian education whose goal is to train Christians of all ages to fulfill their basic biblical functions in the church. The movement in all denominations from a static to a dynamic functional concept of the church is a sign of how much we have in common and a promising portent of future progress toward ecumenical oneness. David Ernsberger has helped us to take another step along that road.

WILLIAM J. DANKER
Editor, Church-in-Mission Series

ACKNOWLEDGMENTS

I am deeply grateful to have been invited to deliver the lectures on which this book is based at Concordia Seminary's eleventh annual Institute of the Church in Mission held in August, 1967. The friendly and generous response of those in attendance was especially gratifying for a Presbyterian who made no secret of his denominational identity before a predominantly Lutheran audience. The experience of the lectures left me with a renewed sense of our oneness in Christ in the midst of our deep mutual respect for confessional integrity.

I would like to express my appreciation to my secretary, Mrs. Robert Abercrombie, who somehow found the time to type the original lectures; to Robert L. Conrad, Director of the Institute, who helped me as correspondent and host; and to William J. Danker, who has assisted me with many of the details involved in publication.

January 1, 1969   D. J. E.

CONTENTS

PREFACE

I believe that there is hope for the local church. Less than a generation ago, such an affirmation would have been greeted with puzzled amusement and perhaps impatience, especially if it had been voiced by a clergyman. Why, of course there's hope! Who ever doubted it? And why are you—a minister at that—talking about "hope" anyway? The local church is doing its job, here and now. The cause of Christ has always been fulfilled by the local congregation of his loyal followers, and it always will be. The future is assured.

There is little point in dwelling on the obvious chasm that separates us today from a time of unfaltering, axiomatic trust in the institution of the local church. To many in today's theological avant-garde, a belief in the traditions and life of the congregation amounts to a nearly heretical arch-conservatism. We are told that the "action"—and the hope—lie elsewhere, out there in the world, in novel experiments on changing frontiers of the secular city, or, currently, in "the underground church." We would be tragically underestimating this challenge if we viewed it as limited to a few highly vocal critics of established institutions. The disillusionment is widespread. Preachers are vacating pulpits to assume secular positions, fewer and fewer seminary students plan to enter the parish ministry, church membership lags behind population growth. Is there, truly, any hope for the local church?

It is not my purpose to present a comprehensive argument for the local church over against proposed experimental forms. Too often the critics put their case in either/or terms; we are not given a both/and option. This restriction appears to be based on the prejudgment that energy expended on a venerable institution resembles flogging a dead horse. But here, I submit, the burden of the argument resides with those who would do away with the local congregation. The needs of our time are so varied and vast that we must use any and every means to fulfill Christ's ministry among men. The local church has proved itself a creative vehicle for that ministry in the past. To be sure, dead tradition is nothing but a burden. But a dynamic tradition, open to change, carries a momentum that can transform human life more widely and lastingly than any mere innovation. We need to test new instruments for communicating the gospel; we need to exploit the untapped potential of older instruments; and we need to keep open the channels for a cross-fertilizing dialogue between new and old.

I believe in the future of the local congregation gathered in the name of Christ because I know, from firsthand experience and from the testimony of others, that it can work. It works to achieve the reconciliation among men and between man and God for which

Christ lived and died. It can *only* work, however, when the church is truly open to the needs and problems of real people in a real world, and when it is equally open to new ways of meeting those needs.

The following chapters represent an effort to open up some possible paths for the local church to follow in fulfilling its mission in our day. It is my intention to be practical and helpful, but I have no illusions about prescribing panaceas for every church in every context. The frequent use of illustrations from my personal parish experience should be understood simply as an attempt to be relevant and concrete by reporting on what I know best—not to extol myself or the congregations I have served; we have had our failures, too.

The movement of the book is from inward concerns to outward mission. It begins by defining the inclusive educational purpose of the church, and then explores the fulfillment of that purpose in preaching, in service within the congregation, the home, and the school, in fellowship and strategic cooperation with other churches, and in the Christian's witness in his daily work.

What hope there is for the local church rests finally in the hands of God, not in man's tinkering with institutional machinery. To forget this is to dissipate all our energies in useless striving. The proposals contained in these pages are offered in the spirit which must inform all of our strategies for renewal of the church—that God may reshape and use them to fit his design for his kingdom.

D. J. E

TO BE IS TO TEACH

Why are we here? Where did we come from and where are we going? The simplest questions are often the most difficult to answer and, therefore, the most frequently avoided. This is no less true for the church than for the individual or for any institution. John W. Meister, an experienced and thoughtful parish pastor, indicts and challenges nearly every local congregation with a down-to-earth observation:

It seems to me that the church in our generation suffers its most shocking lack of power from the failure of particular churches to define their reason for being. Our denomination's committees on ministerial relations frequently have cause to guide the officers of a local church in filling out a four-page "Church Information Form." The first three pages are concerned with statistical information, and the facts are generally forthcoming with little effort. The last page leads off with this question: "What is the particular mission of your particular church?" I have sat in many of these sessions with church officers and never yet have they been able to answer this question with intelligence and conviction. Most often they are like the Ephesians in their ignorance of the Holy Spirit's existence—they do not even know that there is such a thing as a mission for the local church. When our committee prods the officers for an answer, about the most we can hope for is, "to minister to our people." That much could be said for the Elks Lodge.[1]

This description should not be taken as a criticism of church officers, or of laymen in general, or of this or that congregation or denomination. It applies to every church which fails—and who among us can cast the first stone?—to define and to live out its own reason for being. The need to rethink our purpose and mission is a never-ending task, for men forget and tend to drift into aimlessness. We cannot begin the quest for church renewal in our time until we ask, "Why the church?"

H. Richard Niebuhr repeatedly declared in *The Purpose of the Church and Its Ministry* that the church's purpose could be defined as "the increase among men of love for God and neighbor." Such a definition may strike us as being simple in the extreme; yet it is significant that this conception seems to be in the forefront of contemporary theological reflection about the church and its purpose. The theological word which sums up "the increase of love" is reconciliation. In the Presbyterian Confession of 1967, reconciliation between God and man, and the consequent gift and imperative of reconciliation among men, is the dominant concept. In the words of the Preface:

God's reconciling work in Jesus Christ and the mission of reconciliation to which He has called His church are the heart of the gospel in any age. Our generation stands in peculiar need of reconciliation in Christ. Accordingly this Confession of 1967 is built upon that theme.[2]

2

Indeed, everything that is declared in this Confession concerning the reality of the church is subsumed in Part II under the heading "The Ministry of Reconciliation." Speaking of the mission of the church, the Confession declares:

> To be reconciled to God is to be sent into the world as his reconciling community. This community, the church universal, is entrusted with God's message of reconciliation and shares his labor of healing the enmities of mankind. Christ has called the church to this mission and given it the gift of the Holy Spirit.

The church exists because of and for the sake of the Word of God. That is to say, the church was created by God's Word and exists to proclaim it. The primary task of the church as the corporate servant of the Word is to communicate both the *promise* and the *reality* of reconciliation, which is the heart of the Word. Indeed, it can be said that reconciliation to one's real self, to others, and to God is *the* business of the church, an inclusive definition of its reason for being. As the new covenant community created by God's Spirit, the church is set in the world to bring the gift of God's reconciliation to man in the midst of his alienation and estrangement. It is only logical to affirm, then, that this reconciling purpose provides a criterion for all the activities of the church. As George F. MacLeod, of the Church of Scotland's Iona Community, has expressed it:

> The serious week-day business of a congregation is to create the apparatus for the exercise of reconciliation: reconciliation to each other because God has reconciled us to Himself in Jesus Christ.[3]

3

Similarly, Reuel Howe sets reconciliation as the central standard for the evaluation and ordering of parish life:

> Some of the superficial and irrelevant concerns of church life are due to the absence of an effective criterion by which we may evaluate our individual and corporate witness. Reconciliation is one of the key words for understanding the purpose of the Christian ministry, which belongs as much to the laity as to the clergy.[4]

Reconciliation in Christ—that is the gospel, the message we bear from God to men. And this is a reconciliation God has already wrought, not a task we must start from scratch. It follows that our essential business in the church is not to satisfy or "reconcile" God, nor is it to plead for his blessing, mercy, and forgiveness for man, nor is it to seek his acceptance; it is not to lead others to seek his acceptance by means of spiritual exercises of one kind or another, or by psychic experiences, good works, or moral living; it is not for us to redeem man, individually or socially, nor is it to "save the world." Rather, we must say that whatever the changing cultural forms the church must adopt for its ministry in different contexts, our sole task in the twentieth century or in any other century is *to communicate the gospel*. It is to convey by any means at our disposal the Good News that sin *is* forgiven, that man *has been* reconciled to God by the atoning life and death of Jesus Christ, and to summon people to repentance and faith in this once-for-all atonement, so that they may become in fact what they are in principle through God's reconciling intention and action toward

4

them. It follows that, prior to all questions of order, policy, strategy, budget, and program, *communication* is the basic and essential work of ministry in the church. Whatever is done, whatever means are used, all that the church does should be for the single purpose of making known in and to the world this atoning and reconciling act of God in Jesus Christ.

Communication of the gospel is, of course, the chief function of Christian education. The educational mission of the church must be recognized as having central and pervasive significance in every aspect of congregational life. It is noteworthy that contemporary definitions of Christian education contain striking parallels to systematic theologians' definitions of the purpose of the church; both give a central place to the concept of redemptive relationships and the work of reconciliation. Lewis J. Sherrill's definition is representative. He writes:

Christian education is the attempt, ordinarily by members of the Christian community, to participate in and to guide the changes which take place in persons in their relationships with God, with the Church, with other persons, with the physical world, and with one's self.[5]

Because of the new emphasis on Christian education as a function of interpersonal relationships, Christian educators during recent years have begun to see their work in larger terms. They have been making increasing use of such phrases as "the teaching church," or "the church as teacher," or "church education." But the conception of the nature and function of the church which underlies these phrases is not of recent origin. It is implicit in the emphasis of Reformed theology on the primacy of the teaching and preaching roles of the clergy, an emphasis which can be traced back explicitly to the writings of such Reformed theologians as John Calvin and Richard Baxter. Calvin begins the fourth book of his *Institutes of the Christian Religion*, in which he elaborates his doctrine of the church, by describing the church as a mother and a teacher. He abruptly drops the "mother" metaphor and concentrates on describing the church in its entirety as a school of doctrine; the primary function of the church is to be a teacher, a guardian, a guide.

Calvin does not confine this teaching function to children and youth; no adult ever outgrows his need for the "school of Christ."

> Our infirmity will not admit of our dismission from her school; we must continue under her instruction to the end of our lives. . . . We see that God, who might perfect His people in a moment, chooses not to bring them to manhood in any other way than by the education of the church.[6]

Calvin's ideal of the church as a school of Christian doctrine in which everyone, regardless of age, should continue to grow included an ideal concerning the functions of the clergy. Calvin believed that the primary if not the exclusive function of the ministry was to give instruction in apostolic doctrine. This same conception of the church as a teacher is echoed over a century later in Richard Baxter's *The Reformed Pastor:*

> All Christians are the disciples or scholars of Christ: the church is His school: we are His ushers: the Bible is His grammar: this it is we must be daily teaching them.[7]

To regard the church primarily as a teacher is not to belittle the importance of its other functions as an evangelistic, witnessing, worshiping community, any more than regarding the clergyman primarily as an educator minimizes the importance of his other functions. Rather, it means subsuming all functions of the church and its ministry under the unifying category of the communication of the gospel of reconciliation. The church as communicator of the gospel, as God's ordained agent of continuing revelation, is a teaching church in everything it does. It is this task of communication which most centrally characterizes and describes the apostolic obligation of the church.

The emphasis on the church as teacher, and a correlative stress on the centrality of the educational ministry, finds contemporary support in the growing recognition that the church *inevitably* teaches. Education *of some sort* goes on wherever and whenever any portion of the church is functioning in any way. The curriculum of Christian education really resides in all the activities the church provides, uses, or recognizes for guiding the growth of persons in their relationships to God, the church, other persons, and themselves. Thus worship, preaching, study groups, service enterprises, social fellowship, social action, and even recreation are

7

included in this broad concept of Christian education, and must be considered in any adequate analysis of the educational function of the local church.

We cannot choose *whether* we shall provide educational opportunities; we can only choose what *kind* we shall have. This truth is well stated by Donald W. Crawford:

> The parish fellowship communicates its faith by the quality of the living relationships existing among its people, that is, by the kind of conviction shown in the way they accept one another in their common worship and work. The parish itself is constantly "teaching" its religion irrespective of what may be said from the pulpit, in the classroom, in the study course, or in the lecture series. . . . Something is always being communicated to people through the parish fellowship, whether consciously directed through formal effort or as a result of the unconscious impact of the parish people upon each other.[8]

Thus the contemporary emphasis on a theological understanding of the church as teacher both affirms and goes beyond the seventeenth- and eighteenth-century Reformed conception of the church as teacher, especially as articulated in Reformed theology. Within the traditional Reformed view, the educational aspect of every major function of the church was recognized, but there was a tendency to regard the communication of the gospel, the task of Christian education, as essentially a verbal matter, rather than part of the complex web of interpersonal relationships. The ministry of the Word often was defined too literally as a ministry of words. Commenting on this historical phenomenon, Hendrik Kraemer has observed:

> The extravagant and nearly exclusive stress on verbal communication, on preaching and sermonizing, in the world of the churches, which issued from the Reformation, was a degeneration or distortion of the Reformers' rediscovery of the prophetic character and quality of the Word of God. This stress has closed the eyes of the church to the manifold means of communication which we find in the Bible, which in contradiction to our western world is not confined to, or imprisoned in, a "verbal culture." . . . The Christian message, which must be communicated, has such deep and wide dimensions that they transcend the territory of verbal culture, howsoever refined and high its standard may be.[9]

Assuming that these insights are essentially valid, it follows that a church's program of Christian education must reflect an awareness of the crucial importance of redemptive and reconciling experiences in the nurturing process. Our criteria for evaluating that program will be directed to the quality of interpersonal relations in every aspect of parish life. That life together we have in the church is the "curriculum" of our Christian education. Each congregation should undertake a self-evaluation which will reveal the impact of this total curriculum. Perhaps the following questions can help to launch a reappraisal of a local church's educational posture—and of that church's reason for being.

(1) What means does your parish board have of evaluating the integrity of doctrine in what is actually being communicated in men's and women's groups, youth groups, church school, etc.?

9

(2) What means does your parish board employ for evaluating the *effectiveness* of what is communicated? That is, do we have a way of knowing what is actually retained, experienced, and incorporated integrally within a wider framework of learning, so that sacred and secular knowledge are effectively correlated in the minds of church people? This kind of correlation is essential if the laity is to relate its citizenship in the church to its citizenship in the world. The Presbyterian Confession of 1967 recognizes the importance of this dual focus, declaring that ". . . effective preaching, teaching, and personal witness require disciplined study of both the Bible and the contemporary world." How are these two objects of Christian study, the Bible and the contemporary world, functionally related in your educational program? What types of educational testing do you employ for evaluating how effectively the two are linked? Are these evaluations subsequently fed back to church teachers to guide them into more effective ways of communication?

(3) How are various adult groups, other than classes or study groups, structurally related to the Christian education committee and its work of planning and policy formation? All types of interpersonal relationships in parish life have some sort of educational impact; all groups help or hinder the communication of the gospel of reconciliation. How are these groups, whose primary purpose may not have been considered to be education, given program resources of educational value?

(4) In the light of the evidence of growing alienation between the "now" generation and older people, what opportunities are provided for a reconciling dialogue between youth and adults? In addition to classes and study groups spanning the generations, are there also efforts to involve youth with adults in policy and planning functions? Is there provision in the life of the church for dialogue between men and women concerning their often divergent and conflicting understandings of their respective roles in church, home, and community life? Is there an opportunity for airing controversial issues centered in some of the major social problems of our time? How is such controversy, which is often politely hidden, illuminated and aired for educational purposes, and thus opened for the Spirit's healing and reconciling activity in your midst?

(5) What part does Christian education play in your program of evangelism? How does the church seek to equip its entire membership educationally for the task of evangelism? How does it equip those who have been specially designated for this task?

(6) In considering the church's functions as a gathered community both of worship and of learning, what relation do you see between worship in primarily educational groupings, such as the church school and the youth fellowship, and formal worship in the sanctuary? In what ways does the Sunday morning service provide, either regularly or occasionally, for the religious needs of people of various ages attending worship as family units at one time

11

and place? In what ways does the regular morning worship accommodate itself to the developmental needs of children and youth, with content applicable to their concerns and their levels of experience? What provision is made to help members of choirs to perceive their function as a ministry, to grow in knowledge of hymnology and other ecclesiastical music history, and to appreciate the symbolic meanings behind the words they sing? What provisions are made to relate the content of preaching to the content of teaching in the parish?

(7) How are the social or recreational functions of groups within the church related to the process of religious nurture, if at all? As measured by the criterion of God's will for reconciliation in human fellowship, do all the social and recreational activities within the parish seem appropriate and helpful? Are some more valid than others? Are some so selective or arbitrarily exclusive that they are inimical to the gospel?

(8) The Presbyterian Confession of 1967 makes this interesting observation concerning the ministry of the laity in the world:

> The church disperses to serve God wherever its members are, at work or play, in private or in the life of society. . . . Their witness is the church's evangelism. Their daily action in the world is the church in mission to the world. The quality of their relations with other persons is the measure of the church's fidelity. Each member is a deputy of the church endowed by the Spirit with some gift of ministry and is responsible for

the integrity of his witness in his own particular situation. He is entitled to the guidance and support of the Christian community. . . .

How does the church support, affirm, and guide its people in their dispersed life in the world (a) in regard to their daily work as homemakers or breadwinners, (b) in terms of their political and cultural involvements in the community, and (c) in creative stewardship of their leisure opportunities as individuals and as families? In particular, what provision is made for the nurture and guidance of the laity in their Christian ministry as parents?

None of these questions is easy to answer. However, they are not asked rhetorically, as if no answer were expected or even possible. They are all answerable, and in creatively affirmative ways. Indeed, the affirmative answers that can be given are a measure of the fidelity which, by the grace of God, the church with all its frailty can achieve.

Some proposals for response are given in the following chapters in the form of suggestions and examples that have proved helpful in certain concrete situations. Chapter two, on the relation of preaching and teaching in the church, explores ways of evaluating the effectiveness of communication, the educational use of controversy in the church, and the relationship between worship and learning. The third chapter indicates some methods of encouraging dialogue among adults and between adults and youth on their roles in the church, home, and community life. The fourth chapter suggests how cooperative clusters of churches can meet some challenges that are far beyond the capacity of any single congregation. The last of the major questions I have posed here, on training the laity for ministry in their vocational world, is discussed in the final chapter. It is my hope that some of the suggestions will be found to have relevance in different contexts and that they may stimulate imaginative response in other local churches.

PREACHING FOR RENEWAL

"The proof of the divinity of our gospel," Woodrow Wilson once observed, "is the preaching it has survived." As the son of a Presbyterian minister, Wilson was in a reasonably good position to know. There is little doubt that our gospel has survived some pretty poor preaching down through the centuries. Surely that should give us all today the courage to go on Sunday after Sunday: the gospel will probably survive our sermons too. But poor preaching is not really the heart of our problem. Even what might be called "great preaching" seems often to have very poor results in moving its lay hearers into vital involvement in the church's mission. Preaching seems to us to have been far more effective during the Reformation and in earlier periods of the church's history. Is this because our preaching of the gospel is not as good as that of former ages? Is it because preaching pales by comparison with the impact of television and movies on our people in this "Age of McLuhan"? Or is it because our services of worship, especially our preaching, are so largely unrelated to other aspects of both the religious and the secular life of our hearers? I am strongly inclined to believe that this latter factor lies near the root of the problem. I am very much in sympathy with the layman who remarked that he was sick and tired of being talked to as if he were a Corinthian.

In this chapter, I intend to propose some ways in which preaching might result in more effective teaching, in a more wholehearted orientation of people's lives into the postures of mission. Speaking of the tradition of the earliest period of the Protestant Reformation, church historian Wilhelm Pauck has reminded us:

> Early Protestant preaching was doctrinal and became more and more so. . . . It was the duty of the reformers and of the early Protestant ministry to inculcate right Christian teaching and "pure doctrine" in the minds of men. This is why as *preachers* they were primarily *teachers.*[1]

The tradition of doctrinal and expository preaching has been prominent in mainstream Protestant churches since the Reformation, and most pastors are keenly aware of the teaching values that are at least potentially inherent in preaching. But many ministers seem insensitive to the mutually supportive relationship that can exist between preaching as a teaching method and other methods of teaching, of motivating and guiding changes in the behavior and attitudes of the people of God. I have in mind particularly opportunities for dialogue directly related to the content of preaching. I think it is noteworthy that when our Lord spoke to the disciples or to the multitudes for any length of time he would usually follow up with discussions permitting dialogue with his hearers. We find this same pattern of preaching followed by dialogue in the record of the apostolic preaching found in the Book of Acts. Both Christ and his apostles evidently were aware that preaching by itself had limitations as a teaching method, as a means of facilitating redemptive change, and they realized the importance of discussing what had been preached.

The central emphasis of this chapter is on the power of the sermon when it both begins and eventuates in dialogue. A number of examples from concrete parish situations are intended to show how teaching and preaching may be more effectively combined so that they may support each other in the task of communicating the gospel. First are some instances of sermons eventuating in dialogue, followed by examples of creative experimentation in the less familiar practice of using dialogue preceding the sermon to help shape the sermon.

Probably the most well-known and widespread form of following up the preaching experience with dialogue is the after-service discussion group, which increasing numbers of churches are inaugurating. Such groups usually meet immediately after a service, encouraging fresh and spontaneous reactions of the laity to what was expounded in the service, and expression of their personal feelings about how adequately the preacher's message elaborated the full and true meaning of God's Word to his people. There are a number of churches which have such groups after worship or between two services, on a regular year-round basis; other churches provide for such reaction groups only on special occasions and during certain seasons.

For a number of years while he was pastor of the First Congregational Church of West Haven, Connecticut, Dr. Gerald Jud conducted a creative program along these lines during Lent. Dr. Jud had organized his congregation geographically into neighborhood groups called "colonies." The Lenten sermons he preached were mimeographed in advance and each was distributed to the congregation following the service on the Sunday it was delivered. The contents of the sermon provided the basis for discussion when the "colonies" gathered in homes during the following week. Thus, the message of the sermon was not only heard but read, reflected upon, and discussed. During two Lenten seasons, I have followed a similar pattern of midweek discussion based on a sermon series, with one major addition, that of readings from a basic book related to the sermon series, thus amplifying the common experience and exposure upon which dialogue in the group was based.

A similar pattern was used a few years ago in an election year when I was preaching a short series on the social and ethical teachings of my denomination. Because Christian social ethics are a matter of profound controversy and misunderstanding in the church today, it is difficult for any preacher to be either fair or effective as a communicator of the gospel unless he provides an opportunity for lay people to react to a presentation

of the issues or of their denomination's social teachings. The dialogue at times became quite heated, as
one might expect. But the most striking result was that
conservatives and liberals were truly listening to one
another for the first time. And the positions adopted
by the denomination, whether agreed with fully or not,
were seen by virtually everyone participating as being
at least rooted in scriptural affirmations concerning
justice and compassion. Preaching which seeks to relate the mercy and judgment of God to great ethical
issues of the day, such as peace, poverty, and racial
justice, can be and often is helpful to those in the pews;
but just as often, such preaching by itself, isolated from
any wrestling with the issues in discussion among lay
members, can be a means of escape from a truly prob-
ing and vigorous application of the Christian gospel
to the layman's arena of public responsibility.

The findings of many opinion polls and sociological
studies substantiate the assertion that one-way means
of communication are relatively ineffective in changing
people's attitudes and opinions on social questions.
Preaching resembles a one-way street in most churches
today, and preachers need to ask themselves how often
their hearers change in a direction that reflects any
profound awareness of the universal mercy and love
of God. Resounding manifestos and pronouncements
emanating from official boards and distant delegated
assemblies of the denominations, and even prophetic
preaching itself, can be simply irrelevant to the Christian social witness. They become relevant only when
they stimulate creative dialogue among laymen who

are seeking in a disciplined manner to determine the mind of Christ on the great questions of the day. Only by creating more opportunities for significant dialogue can we hope to narrow the vast gulf separating the social-ethical convictions of clergy from those of the laity, and the enormous disparity between the national pronouncements of the churches and the attitudes of the man in the pew. Reuel L. Howe, Director of the Institute for Advanced Pastoral Studies, in Bloomfield Hills, Michigan, bears testimony to the effectiveness of this sermon-discussion method:

> Our experience at the Institute reveals that the quality of listening of a whole congregation, and therefore of their participation in the preaching of the Church, can be changed by fairly consistent use of sermon discussion groups in which half a dozen or more people discuss the sermon and its meaning for them. . . . Ministers who have employed this kind of resource observe that even the behavior of a congregation changes with the increase of dialogue between pulpit and pew. They acknowledge that they experience a sense of liberation in their preaching as a result of the relationship that is born out of the dialogue. . . . This makes a sermon a living event instead of an oratorical performance, an event which becomes a part of the action of God in the world. It is an event in which clergy and laity have a mutual and complementary responsibility. Furthermore, the process of this concept of preaching shares in the nature of Christian relationship which is to be understood as a relationship in which each person calls forth the power of being of another. The minister as preacher calls forth the parishioner as a questioning, affirming Christian person, and the parishioner calls forth the minister as a person who is the instrument of the truth of God for others.[2]

To follow preaching with dialogue groups is only one way, the more common and well-known way, of transforming monologue into dialogue in which clergy and laity may mutually support and enable each other for their respective Christian ministries. The hour of worship itself may be enriched, the act of preaching may be made intrinsically more relevant, when it issues out of dialogue between clergy and laity as the people of God, *preceding* and hence helping to shape the sermon itself. I can illustrate this method first from my own parish experience, and then from the experience of two other parishes.

For a number of years, I delivered an expository sermon each month on the particular Scripture passage which was the basis of study in the monthly meetings of the women's circles. During the week preceding this sermon, I would meet with the women who were responsible for leading the discussion in their circles that month. We would discuss the Scripture passages for about an hour and a half, so that they went to their circles prepared with any information I could provide concerning these passages from my preparation for the sermon. Thus, each was prepared to function as a discussion leader or resource person just as effectively as I could—probably more effectively, because laymen can often communicate more clearly with one another than with the pastor. More important, my dialogue with these leaders contributed immeasurably to my own understanding of the study passage. Advance discussion revealed to me common areas of misunderstanding and confusion and questioning, so that when

I went to compose my sermon after such a preliminary meeting, I would be seeking to answer real questions. I also had the benefit of their insights into Scripture meanings that I might otherwise have missed. The discussion with the women actually helped to form the sermon, to make it not an arid monologue but a lively exchange addressing itself to questions which people had actually asked. Too often we are tempted in our preaching to answer questions which no one is asking or concerned about.

A more creative example of this general method is given in the parish ministry of Dr. Browne Barr, formerly Professor of Homiletics at Yale Divinity School and now pastor of the First Congregational Church of Berkeley, California.[3] Dr. Barr's plan involves a much larger proportion of the members of his congregation in weekly rather than monthly discussion with him, seeking together to respond to the text for the sermon of the week. This weekly discipline has become a vital part of Dr. Barr's background work preliminary to sermon writing. It has become an equally vital part of the preparation of the participating laymen to hear the Word as it comes to them through Scripture and sermon. Thus, it is a means of implementing the Reformation emphasis and insight to which we pay lip service, that the whole people of God are called to read, study, and respond in community to the meaning of Scripture. Although the writing of the sermon remains the minister's task alone, his insights into the text are amplified and enriched as parishioners share with him their interpretation of the passage. The program had its inception in the fall of 1962 with an invitation extended to members of the congregation through the church bulletin. The announcement read:

> Anyone who is interested in discussing the problems of faith and life and joining others in prayer is invited to meet with the minister in the reception room from 8:30 to 9:30 P.M. on Wednesday. This is not another activity to support.

No specific commitment is asked of participants as a qualification for membership in the group. People simply are invited to return each week. The passage which the group studies each week is the text for the following Sunday's sermon. It is suggested that each member prepare for each meeting by reading the assigned Bible passages, and occasionally commentaries. Participants are also encouraged to bring with them various translations of the Bible, together with their own questions, ideas, and personal needs suggested by the passages. The membership of the group remains open; preliminary Bible reading is encouraged but not mandatory.

Each weekly session of the seminar is led by the minister who is scheduled to preach the following Sunday. Customarily, he introduces the text by sketching briefly the historical and contextual situation in which it was written. Then he gives just enough simple exegesis to indicate where the crucial problems lie and to guard against a gross misreading of the text. He may explain briefly his reason for choosing the text or theme, its place in the Christian year, or its relation to some pressing concern in the life of the community or the parish to which the sermon is intended to be addressed and focused. Sometimes he concludes by proposing a question designed to center the discussion on some specific area or to initiate the process of free association in the small-group settings which follow. These matters then are responded to for thirty-five minutes in round-table groups of eight to ten persons, which then feed back their insights to the total group. From the end of his opening presentation until the close of the meeting, the preacher of the week remains, for the most part, a silent listener, taking notes on the responses of the people. He usually circulates among the round-table groups, but tries to stay on the fringe, listening.

The contribution this experience makes to a sense of fellowship and mutual involvement in the ministry of proclamation is enormous. The preacher of the week often is the grateful recipient of profound observations which bring depth of insight. No less significant are what might seem at first to be trivia, small human touches that creep into the discussion and serve to enlarge the sermon's range of interest, providing the preacher with bridges for reaching the people at points that are realistic and familiar to them. Such contributions come from unexpected sources. One sermon which college students received with particular gratitude was made lively and relevant for them through subtle use of an incident recounted quite casually by a well-to-do, retired, conservative member of the group with whom the college crowd would have thought they had little in common.

47439

Preliminary discussion in Browne Barr's church has served to increase receptivity and ease tensions when sermons have dealt with controversial issues. The expressed consensus among lay people about the ambiguity of moral decisions prevented one sermon-in-the-making from missing its mark completely. Again and again the seminar contributes vital touches of realism to the developing sermon. Often, as the group confronts the text, new themes emerge which call for treatment in later sermons. Thus, in many and varied ways the church's preaching is enriched and the Scriptures opened more widely to an unusually involved and expectant people.

The seminar is enlarged during the Lenten period, when the number of participants increases from 35 to between 150 and 200 (out of a congregation of approximately 1600). Fifteen minutes of radio time scheduled on a local station enables the minister and organist to reach parishioners gathered in groups in neighborhood homes. Here the people follow the broadcast exegesis of the text, join as they wish in the singing of a hymn, unite in prayer, and then continue with living-room seminars for forty-five minutes. Each year this has led to a lively sense of the unity of the congregation, even in its geographical dispersion. The leaders meet in advance to prepare for these neighborhood sessions, and each leader is responsible for forwarding a summary of expressed insights to the minister, often by coming to his home after the meeting. One section meets in the church at seven in the morning for a chapel service, a simple breakfast, and the seminar.

An even higher proportion of members in a much smaller congregation—in fact nearly all the members— take part in sermon preparation for a Presbyterian church in a Minneapolis suburb.[4] This church is built entirely upon a cellular structure of small units called "apostles' groups" which select their own subject matter, time, frequency, and place of meeting. When a number of new members are received into the church, they are formed into a new "apostles' group." During the eight-week period preceding Easter in 1966, all the "apostles' groups" gathered weekly for a study of what was then the Proposed Confession of 1967, which has since been adopted by the Presbyterian General Assembly. By Thursday morning of each week, the groups turned in to the pastor for his sermon preparation the questions and comments which emerged in the dozen or so "apostles' groups." Each Sunday's sermon was based upon the section of the Confession studied during the preceding week. This made possible an effective dialogue, not only between pulpit and pew, but also among nearly all adult members of this congregation.

However great or small the proportion of those involved in dialogue with the pastor either before or following the worship experience, the sermon must never be regarded as the final word. "Exposition" means literally an opening up, an exposing, not a definitive closing and wrapping-up of a subject. A sermon is properly somewhat analogous to a lawyer's brief. Christian preaching is preaching for a verdict, the pleading of a case, a call for a decision. Whatever the inherent limitations in its effectiveness, and admittedly there are many, preaching is the one way in which the call to mission, the call for an about-face from ingrown concerns and outward toward the world, may be heard by everyone in the church. It is the one means by which virtually all persons in the church are forced to make a choice, to say either yes or no to the Word of God. That Word calls them to a discipleship to be exercised not only within ecclesiastical structures, but also, and even primarily, within the secular order. Preaching on the issue of lay ministry and the consequent call for the renewal of the church's mission to the world creates a moment of judgment for all who hear it. It says, in effect: Behave yourself according to the divine privilege and calling in which you stand and are set, or else acknowledge before God your inner unbelief. Accept your call to ministry implicit in the fact of your baptism and membership in Christ's church, or else have the honesty to repudiate it. "Choose this day whom you will serve" (Josh. 24:15).

The fellowship of dialogue is likely to involve only a relative few. Obviously, the direct confrontation of the whole membership therefore occurs only through preaching. Thus, whatever the intrinsic shortcomings of this means of communication as compared with the experience of dialogue, preaching can always put across the necessity of making some decision about the total and inclusive Christian call to mission. The summons to decision concerning this call should be implicit in preaching. Preaching on this subject, as on any other, properly begins with what God has done and is doing, as Scripture—and present events perceived in the light of Scripture—bear witness. Only then can preaching indicate what men should decide to be and to do in response to God's gracious activity. Therefore, biblical preaching at its best begins not by dispensing abstract principles and ideals but by pointing to God's action as revealed in biblical history, and then, by logical extension from this ancient revelation, pointing to indications of his present action in human events.

One of the chief functions of preaching is to help people see that God is already at work in their world. Too many are prone to think that he acts only within the gathered fellowship of the church, only when two or three are gathered in his name, and not when those same two or three are scattered in the world in his name. Preaching should help them to see not only what God is already doing but also what *they* may already be doing in his world even without being theologically conscious of it, as co-creators with God and as ambassadors or agents of his reconciling work among men.

In Jesus' Parable of the Last Judgment, the righteous are dumbfounded when they are told that they have been serving Christ in the secular fact of their kindnesses to their fellowmen. This is also a parable for lay people today, who have a great need for enlightenment and inspiration concerning the ultimate sacredness of many of their secular commitments and actions. They must be told who they already are within the divine economy, that they already are God's ministers and priests by virtue of their membership in the church, however faithlessly they may presently be regarding or performing this priesthood, this ministry. Only when they see what they already are in principle can it be fruitful to challenge them to become such ministers in fact. Biblical faith first testifies to what is, and only then does it become power for the accomplishment of what ought to be. It declares how things presently stand between God and man, before it introduces the exhortation, the "therefore," of appropriate Christian response.

A sermon is not intended to result simply in discussion, valuable as this may be, but to bring forth action. In Jesus' Parable of the Sower, the purpose of the sowing is to bring forth a fruitful harvest. The seeds that sprouted up quickly and then withered away because they were not rooted deeply enough are like truths that take temporary hold in our minds but do not grow. Truth must always be related to action. Truth cannot flourish in our minds unless it constantly renews itself in our experience. The sermon, therefore, is not finished when the preacher leaves the pulpit. When the sermon has been delivered, the church, thus far, has only half preached it; only the pastor's part is completed. The rest of the preaching takes place when the people apply what they have heard in the pulpit in their lives as they go out into the world. As the English Congregationalist theologian P. T. Forsyth once said, "The first business of the individual preacher is to enable the church to preach."

In this sense, the ideal length of a sermon is not nineteen minutes, as many suppose. A sermon should ideally be infinitely long, as it proceeds from thought to conviction, to commitment and experience. What I have been trying to point to was well summarized three centuries ago in Question 160 of the Westminster Larger Catechism:

Question: What is required of those that hear the Word preached? *Answer:* It is required of those that hear the Word preached that they attend upon it with diligence, preparation, and prayer, examine what they hear by the Scriptures, receive the truth with faith, love, meekness and readiness of mind, as the Word of God, meditate and confer on it, hide it in their hearts and bring forth the fruit of it in their lives.[5]

3

SERVICE WITHIN THE STEEPLE'S SHADOW

In this chapter on training for Christian service, it is my intention to concentrate on those kinds of service which Christians render within the institutional church and within the residential community, hence, figuratively, "within the steeple's shadow." The first section deals with training groups for the laity in terms of specialized vocations which they perform within the institutional structure, such as church school teaching and membership on various church boards. The second section will consider aspects of lay training for what Dr. Elton Trueblood calls "your other vocation" in his book of that title—that primary vocation of the laity implicit in their various duties and opportunities in God's world.

Surely one aspect of training for service which needs considerable rethinking is the preparation of church officers. It is an unfortunately common practice to elect laymen to church offices and to press them into assuming their duties immediately. The achievement of a more mature and informed lay leadership and a more orderly transition between terms of office on various church boards can be encouraged in a simple manner. If a church will arrange its bylaws and procedures so that there is a decent time interval between the election of new officers and their formal assumption of duties, the interim period can be used for intensive lay training. Two or three months before they are installed, officers-elect should be engaged in special training and orientation sessions. This also allows these trainees to attend board meetings as observers, as virtual understudies for the positions they are soon to assume.

Once they are in office, it is often difficult to motivate lay people to attend training conferences and to read suggested books to improve their functioning. Frequently they are so busy performing the actual duties of their position that they feel they have little time to give to growth in proficiency of leadership or in a deeper theological understanding of their part within the total mission of the church. It is axiomatic that an individual's motivation and readiness for learning experiences is likely to be greatest immediately before he assumes some new responsibility, whether that be marriage or a new job or a special assignment. Why not capitalize on this readiness, a readiness which is quite likely to diminish or even vanish once the individual has been installed in his new office?

In our church, we changed the bylaws of the congregation several years ago so that officers for the coming year are now elected eleven weeks before they actually begin their new duties. One of their training experiences during this period is attendance at a weekend retreat devoted to an appraisal of the overall mission of the church. The purpose of this appraisal is to enable each layman to see his task whole, to get the total picture, to appreciate how the particular job he will perform contributes to a coherent unity of mission. This retreat serves to overcome in some measure the curse of overspecialization, the common problem of lack of communication and understanding between the different boards and committees of a church, whose work as the arms and legs and hands of the Body of Christ is so often poorly coordinated. In addition to participating in this retreat, the officers-elect attend two monthly meetings of the boards on which they are to serve. This gives them a feel for the functioning of the board and opens the way for a joint consideration by the existing board and the members-elect of the particular positions and functions they might best be suited to fill when they assume office. A person is likely to be more highly motivated in his service if he feels that his duty is not a matter of arbitrary assignment, but rather the result of mutual consideration in which he himself is directly involved and in which his experience and gifts are measured against specific needs. It is our custom for the officers-elect to withdraw part way through the meeting and join a board member or one of the pastors to analyze the group process and functioning of the board and to receive more specific training.

One aspect of officer training which seems to be sorely neglected in most churches is preparation for the task of lay calling in the parish. Typically, the only training for lay calling given by the churches is for stewardship visitation. I believe we need to give at least as much attention to lay training in making calls which center upon the needs of the person as we do for calls which relate primarily to the needs of the religious institution. There is a particularly helpful lay-training manual on this aspect of church service which we have used for several years: *How to Make Pastoral Calls: A Guide for Laymen,* by Russell L. Dicks.[1] The title itself is significant, implying as it does the pastoral responsibility which laymen have for one another as part of the priesthood of all believers. Dr. Dicks, one of the nation's most prominent leaders in the field of pastoral counseling, wrote this manual as a lay-oriented revision of his earlier book, *You Came Unto Me,* used by seminaries for years in the training of pastors for calling and counseling. The book deals in a helpful way with various types of calls, such as calls on the sick, the bereaved, the shut-in, the senior citizen, the alcoholic, the emotionally disturbed, the newcomer to the community, and the person facing surgery. One of the most helpful aspects of the manual is that it gives actual conversations from such calls, thus providing interesting and highly realistic case studies which the officers-elect can analyze.

With regard to the training of laymen who are called to serve in the church school or as advisers to the youth program or in similar educational responsibilities, I would suggest a similar pattern of pre-service training. Because opportunities for pre-service training normally come at traditional spring and summer teacher institutes, an early fall date for beginning a stated teaching term has much in its favor. Naturally, new teachers and advisers and administrators assume duties whenever replacements become necessary. Nevertheless, the early fall, as the beginning of the program year, is the logical time to begin a teaching term.

Furthermore, if laymen in other areas of lay ministry in the life of the church serve for specific terms of office, why should not those performing the teaching office operate within the same sort of orderly structure? Such a term of service can be renewed year by year, as seems appropriate both to the individual layman and to the committee responsible for appointments. In our church, following the pattern of the public schools, teachers and youth group advisers are canvassed late in the winter to see if they desire to renew their contract—we call it a "covenant"—for another year, beginning with the first of September. We do nothing to discourage a fairly high turnover in our lay staff in Christian education, paralleling the turnover constitutionally required in staggered terms of office on all church boards. Roy Fairchild and J. C. Wynn, in their book *Families in the Church: A Protestant Survey,*[2] presented convincing evidence that families in which husband or wife or both had held official duties in the church's program of Christian nurture had a far clearer idea of their Christian responsibility in family life, were more conscientious communicators of Christian conviction to their children, and were better informed concerning the mutually supportive relationships between church school and home. The evidence from this survey supports the argument that a considerable rate of turnover in the lay leadership of a Christian education program can strengthen more of the laity for their vocation in Christian family life.

Our pre-service training of laymen for Christian education responsibilities parallels the training we give to church board members before their terms of office begin. Early in the spring, workshop sessions are held for recruits on basic teaching methods and on resources and techniques for youth group advisers. At these sessions, general presentations are given on the basic philosophy of the denominational church school curriculum, together with position papers of the denomination and the local church on our philosophy of youth ministry for the adviser trainees. As in the case of the church officer retreat on the mission of the church, our goal is to enable the laymen bearing specific Christian education responsibilities to see their work whole, to see their special functions within the totality of educational mission. Then, paralleling the exposure of board members-elect to the meetings of their respective boards, the new teacher trainees observe church school classes and youth group meetings during the late spring and early summer. Among other obvious advantages, this enables them to decide upon the age level with which they would prefer to work. These expressed preferences become one consideration affecting the assignment of responsibility for the program year beginning in September. A church educators' retreat early in the fall, concentrating on a preview of specific departmental material together with practice in individual and team planning of church school lessons, climaxes the process of pre-service training.

Just as there are parallels between the training of board members and the training of leaders of Christian education in the pre-service period, so also there are parallels with our in-service training. In continuing lay training during actual service, one effective arrangement we follow is the combination of such training with regular meetings on matters of business and procedure. There are two reasons for such an approach. First, there is the simple fact that it is always difficult to get people together for yet another special meeting of any sort. Second, in-service training given in conjunction with a regular meeting of a board or youth-adviser group or church school staff brings theory and practice together; it introduces new ideas in the immediate practical context of the layman's administrative involvement in the life of the church. If the in-service training being given is not relevant to the needs of the laymen in their concrete tasks, this becomes most obvious when such in-service training and procedural meetings are placed back to back. Both laymen and professional church workers can detect any irrelevance in such a pragmatically oriented context. Following this general principle, the first half-hour or so of any board meeting can effectively be devoted in a disciplined way to church officer training. Similarly, the first part of the monthly church school staff meeting could suitably provide presentations in teaching methodology or theological background for curriculum content, prior to dividing for departmental meetings.

As we shift from the arena of the layman's ministry within the immediate ecclesiastical structures to his ministry outside these structures, it is evident that the greatest single common denominator is family life. Other lay functions in the world have almost infinite degrees of specialization. But only a relatively small proportion of the laity live entirely outside the orbit of primary or at least secondary family responsibilities. Laymen need to perceive the family as their vocation and ministry, or they will never be likely to perceive anything in their common life as part of their vocation and ministry.

One area of Christian ministry where parents frequently fail their children is in a neglect of the priestly aspect of this ministry, especially in the failure to give their children a sense of awe and wonder, of reverence and adoration, of worship and devotion. The laity is harangued from the pulpit regularly for their failure as parents, but they are seldom given practical guidance as to how to begin to fulfill this priestly responsibility. In this regard I would like to recommend a very helpful resource used in one of the Lenten family night courses in our church several years ago, entitled *Opening the Door for God,* a manual for parents by Herman J. Sweet.[3] In addition to providing helpful prayers and a coherently connected program of family Bible reading and reflection, this manual deals realistically with some of the chief hesitancies and obstacles hindering family devotional life. Of course, one of the most formidable obstacles is the lack of satisfactory devotional resources for families. A great number of families in our church have recently been helped by an excellent new resource which I would recommend for families with younger children, for whom there has been a conspicuous lack of materials that are not condescending or full of maudlin sentiment or questionable theology. This new resource, *Let's Talk About God,* comes from the pen of an imaginative Christian educator, Gertrude Ann Priester.[4] The book consists of very short stories about typical childhood experiences and includes an imaginary dialogue between a parent and child concerning the experience. The dialogue helps to articulate the Christian significance of the experience, often in explicit biblical terms, and leads into a simply phrased concluding prayer. The dialogue within the stories easily becomes an opening for dialogue within the family circle.

Another area of need in strengthening parents for the Christian vocation of family life centers in the problem of the rapidly changing role of women in our culture. In the more static, patriarchal, rural-oriented culture of yesteryear, a woman's Christian ministry, her distinctive role, could be simply summed up in the German expression, *"Kinder, Küche und Kirche."* Today, of course, it is far more complex than that, and constantly changing. It may be that women in the church understand more about missionary outreach in this nation and abroad than about *their own mission* as Christian women. A bewildering array of clamant voices beckons them in contradictory directions, and the simpler solutions which satisfied their grandmothers will not suffice for them.

One way to handle this problem is to attack it directly, to deal with it deliberately and explicitly as the theme for a vocational concern group called together to consider what it means to be a woman in Christ. A few years ago, pursuing this direct approach, our church held a series of four monthly seminar meetings on the changing role of women. A handful of especially interested and concerned women of the congregation served as a bibliographical resource group, looking over both secular and religious materials for group study. The book chosen as the basic resource was Gibson Winter's *Love and Conflict*,[5] supplemented by other readings of the bibliographical resource group and reprints of an article, "Growing Up Female," by psychiatrist Bruno Bettelheim.[6] The fact that women in the pilot group had read widely in other sources greatly contributed to the discussions carried out under their leadership in small groups. The small-group sessions followed my lectures on the biblical basis of female identity and responsibility. I tried to overcome my considerable handicaps in instructing women as to what it means to be a woman in Christ by confining my lectures to biblical and theological foundations, relying on the members to bring a witness of shared illumination and insight to one another. A number of women were profoundly supported and helped to new visions of their unique ministry in family and community life.

During the following year we offered a series on the role of women within the structures of the church. Unlike the earlier series, this was truly controversial and explosive; many women gave vent to some of their resentments concerning condescension and subjugation to male authority within ecclesiastical structures. The prevailing pattern of male dominance in our congregation remains largely unshaken in the wake of this series, but questions raised about many assumptions and customs continue to be asked, and, in time, more significant institutional changes may result.

Christian dialogue concerning the woman's role in home, community, and church life does not require the direct, explicit, topical approach. Family-life education can be going on all the time in study groups involving women. Like the prophet Hosea, and like their Lord Jesus in so many of his parables, women tend to perceive divine realities in analogies to family relationships because these are both most familiar and most important to them. In applying the Scriptures to life they seem to seek first to bring them into family life. The expression of "the woman's viewpoint" can bring a wealth of biblical insight concerning the vocation of parenthood, of marriage, and of all family life.

Very few churches, no matter how small they may be, serve only one definable neighborhood. Nearly all churches serve at least a handful of fairly distinguishable neighborhoods from which their constituent members come. For this reason, there is a special value in neighborhood groupings to assist laity in the vocation of Christian family life. The house-church scheme, under which people are gathered by neighborhood groups (or zone groups, as they are sometimes called), is a particularly relevant matrix for lay training because of the importance of the immediate social and economic and cultural environment in the shaping of our life together as families. Many of those who have experimented with this form of vocational concern group have found it a far more effective means of touching people's daily lives in households and neighborhoods than programs which have their geographical focus in the church building. Where there is a wide diversity of neighborhoods served by one church, family-life education groups drawn from the scattered parish frequently find that the geographical distances between different neighborhood settings often entail handicapping psychological distances between participants. The gathering of house-churches or zone groups can also perform an important Christian service to the wider community by helping to form a viable community structure, creating and strengthening lines of communication in neighborhood networks all around the parish where previously little or no true community existed. This in itself would be a significant Christian witness and service in a new suburban development or any area characterized by a high level of transiency, where there is an absence of community feeling. In addition, a regional community of interest and neighborhood friendship might prove to be a more cohesive and significant common bond than a community of interest based upon the coincidences of children's ages within a geographically scattered parish area. The problems of family life today cannot be discussed meaningfully without reference to the external social forces which impinge upon the family. We need to get away from the sentimental illusion of essentially autonomous families sitting around examining the quality of their inner relationships in blissful abstraction from any significant consideration of the environing economic, social, and cultural factors with which they and their children must live.

In this connection, it would be well for Protestants to take a page from the notebook of Roman Catholic experience with their Christian Family Movement in this nation. This movement, which is a part of the renewal movement known as Catholic Action, has as its objective the renewal of Christian family life in its totality through the formation of neighborhood inquiry groups. Nothing that affects the family, whether it be politics, economics, recreation, or art, is foreign to its concern. A Christian Family Movement unit or cell normally consists of four or five neighbor couples who meet alternately at one another's homes. The parish priest serves as chaplain-adviser and consultant for the group. Using the national manual prepared for them, each group follows the three steps which are virtually the model of Catholic Action with regard to all social problems, seeking together to relate the steps to family life: (1) observe a given social situation; (2) judge or evaluate it by Christian doctrinal standards; and then finally (3) take appropriate Christian social action. The program format for a neighborhood meeting includes discussion of passages from the Gospels with guidance from the manual, followed by a period of "social inquiry" set out in the manual lessons and centering upon such topics as economic life, work in modern society, schooling (including school integration and educational provisions for retarded children), sex education in the home, and public health and welfare. Whereas the typical Protestant pattern for family-life education tends to concentrate on matters confined to the private life of the home, such as child-centered psychologizing or how to answer the questions children ask or informal Christian education in the home, the materials prepared by Catholic Action seek to relate questions of family life to the realities of its social milieu. It was these Christian Family Movement groups in our local Roman Catholic parish which were in the vanguard in inaugurating the ecumenical dialogue described in Chapter 4.

The Roman Catholic Church also has much to teach us in another dimension of family-life education—"pre-service" training. It is even more true of family life than of any other responsibility that the time of greatest motivation is the pre-service period of courtship and engagement, not the "in-service" time after the honeymoon is over. The Pre-Cana conferences of the Catholic Church take full advantage of the learning readiness of engaged couples, while Protestants have hardly begun to recognize, much less capitalize on, this potential. Many engaged couples will conscientiously devour every book on the subject of marriage which is shared with them. To undergird this training for that mutual service which is the vocation of Christian marriage, our congregation has over the years developed an extensive premarital counseling collection as part of the regular church library. More books are used in this category than in almost any other. Premarital counseling is sometimes ineffectual because it is used by pastors as an opportunity for monologues or lectures on Christian family life. Reliance on a pastoral counseling library, with titles being selected by engaged couples under pastoral suggestion and direction, allows competent books to do the lecturing. The counselor is then free to listen to a young couple's responses to their reading, in the light of the experience and insight and personality characteristics which they bring to one another.

In most parishes, the second most common vocational denominator, following the service of God within the structures of family life, is the vocation of obtaining an education. To often we have spoken of Christian vocation with children and especially with youth as if this doctrine had only a future reference, a reference to the adult position in society which they will one day assume. The program of Christian nurture in the church should enable children and youth to see that they have a vocation in the present, the vocation of being students to the very best of their ability, in preparation for the faithful exercise of their lifework later on. Even with children who are quite young the church school can help to achieve this sense of vocation by taking the public school curriculum seriously in planning its own program and church school lessons. One of the greatest failings of church education in our time has been its utter abstraction from the secular study in which the child is engaged so many other hours of each week.

Present patterns of church education do not help the child to see his life whole, to see that religious conviction and motivation are closely related to every level of human knowledge and experience. With our tradition of separation of church and state, we cannot expect the public schools to perform this integrative and interpretive function for us. It is the business of the church school to be reasonably well-informed concerning the general curriculum of the public schools in the parish it serves. Specifically, it is the proper function of every department superintendent in the church school to know the syllabus followed in the public school classes of the children in his department; he should see to it that, in lesson-planning and previewing sessions each quarter, specific suggestions are made for the interweaving of secular and sacred knowledge. This is important for the fields of literature and history in particular, but it can often be applied to the sciences and current events studies as well. Any child who sees that his teacher is familiar with his Monday-to-Friday work and correlates it with religious insights will not only begin to see a greater relevance and coherence in the Christian message; he will also indirectly feel himself affirmed by his church in the goodness of those secular learnings he pursues through the week.

An effective way for the church to communicate its conviction of the student's Christian calling at the youth level would be through the general suspension of youth activities during examination periods. Such a step would have meaning and impact only if it were explicitly interpreted to young people as being done in order to affirm in actions, as well as in words, their primary calling under God as students at this point in their lives. It is tragic to note how frequently a church's youth program will needlessly conflict with the scheduling of academic and extracurricular activities in the public schools. If it is true that the primary Christian vocation of young students is to be students, then it is both unfair and self-defeating for the church to force them needlessly into choosing between their school and their church activity simply because the adult leadership has not taken the trouble to consult the school calendar. The way in which the church plans its program ought to communicate to youth the feeling that the church cares about the whole scope of their existence, particularly that rightfully dominant segment of it which is devoted to the educational enterprise. The church should show that it seeks to avoid conflicts with school functions not simply for the institution-centered goal of larger turnouts for its programs but because it desires to uphold its youth in their pursuit of knowledge and skills in the service of the God who is the source of all truth.

A homework retreat for senior highs was conducted in our church to affirm this conviction of Christian calling in student life. It was deliberately scheduled immediately before a major examination period. The purpose of this retreat was to provide an opportunity to study for examinations, and, at the same time, to investigate why and how one studies. This retreat, held over a weekend, included eight to ten hours of time devoted solely to study. In addition, there were presentations by high school educators on subjects such as how to take notes, the psychology of carefully spaced and segmented learning, techniques of effective memorization, and skills in building outlines for written compositions. The pastors were employed in presenting basic theological stimulus material on the Christian task of being a student.

The greatest single evidence of the lack of Christian grace in contemporary student life seems to lie not so much in the sphere of personal morality, about which the older generation is disturbed, as in the sphere of student apathy and distaste for the studies which are their present vocation. Surely one of the greatest challenges to the church's witness to students is the task of helping them to renew their dedication and zest for the task of learning. Many of our young people are not at all sure why they are studying or should study; some who are sure give sub-Christian reasons centering on pride about grades or on the desire for higher social and economic status as an end in itself. The proportion who conceive of studying as their Christian calling would surely be small. Lack of discipline, cheating, apathy, pragmatic single-minded concentration on grades, which are found in varying degrees among young people, are symptoms of the church's failure to stimulate a cogent sense of Christian vocation.

A homework retreat affords an excellent setting for a Christian reevaluation of the ultimate meaning of one's fleeting student years. In addition to dealing with the theological dimensions of vocation, such retreats can take up particular ethical issues confronted in student life, such as cheating, plagiarism, and the giving and receiving of unfair help, as well as such other matters as the value of various extracurricular options in preparing for future service and for leisure fulfillment. Of course, such matters as these can and should be the subject of program topics on other occasions as well; but the environment of study retreat provides a context of especially fertile immediacy for significant conversation on the meaning of one's student years. Those who have participated in retreats of this sort report that, in addition to the value of the dialogue, there is inspiration even in the solitude of the homework sessions. For, in contrast to the loneliness of study in the impersonal atmosphere of a library or in one's room, the corporate discipline of study in the midst of a silent but supportive community and fellowship, one which is concerned not only with learning but also with the ultimate reasons under God for learning, can lead to renewed depth and vigor of commitment.

4

FELLOWSHIP—WITH "OUTSIDERS"?

The New Testament word *"koinonia"* and its usual translation "Christian fellowship" are much used in contemporary parlance about parish life. Generally, this term and its variants are attached exclusively to relations within the local congregation. This seems to be an unwarranted and restrictive limitation of the concept and, indeed, of the possibilities of renewal and mission for the church itself. This chapter will focus on some experiments in Christian fellowship beyond the bounds of the local congregation. The first example is a case study in Protestant–Roman Catholic dialogue that suggests ways of enlarging our notion of "fellowship" to the enrichment of our common life in Christ.

Several years ago, in my former pastorate, the ministers of our church initiated conversations with our counterparts at a Roman Catholic church which happened to face our edifice from the opposite corner of the same intersection. We had heard of interfaith dialogue groups before and we decided that it would be important to try to focus the conversation in a common purpose and effort. We determined that it should be Bible-centered. But correspondence with a special committee of our denomination revealed that at that time they had no knowledge of any Roman Catholic–Presbyterian Bible study on the parish level, or even on an inter-seminary level. We were breaking new ground, and therefore we had to compose our own curriculum of Bible study. Initially, we began by agreeing that the group would consist of six couples, three from each church, together with one priest and one minister as joint resource persons. The Revised Standard Version of the Bible was agreed upon for Old Testament studies, and the New English Bible was to be used for New Testament passages. Each meeting was to begin with devotions, which were composed of readings from the Psalms, classic prayers of Christian antiquity, and portions of a folk mass by Father Clarence Rivers. During the first year, the group met monthly on a rotating basis in the homes of the six lay couples.

The Bible study course developed for the ten monthly meetings was based on central texts that raised such crucial questions as these: In what sense can the church rightfully be called the Body of Christ? What is the nature of the authority given by Christ to Peter in the sixteenth chapter of Matthew? What is meant by Christ's words ascribing to Peter the power of the keys to the kingdom? What is the connection between the Last Supper and the Crucifixion? In what sense is Christ understood to be present in the sacrament of the Lord's Supper? How are all Christians to obey the meaning of what Mary said by the Spirit, "All generations will call me blessed"? Toward the end of the first year of meetings, one monthly session was expanded to expose more people in both parishes to the experience of dialogue. Our curriculum schedule called for an examination of scriptural mandates for racial justice at the May meeting. That month was chosen for the expanded invitational meeting because of the importance of the topic and the need for an ecumenical approach to it. Two parish groups of the Christian Family Movement in the Catholic congregation had been studying this topic and were, therefore, a natural complement for the May meeting of the interfaith group. Their participation would raise the number of Roman Catholic couples to fifteen. Since there was no comparable group already in existence within our church, we invited a dozen other couples who were known to be interested in the subject.

Although the intensity of dialogue present in the smaller continuing group obviously could not be duplicated in the expanded meeting, something of the spirit of trust and respect which had been growing in the previous meetings was communicated to this larger gathering. The experience of this mood was probably more significant than the substance of the passages discussed. No longer was this dialogue group something off in a corner and relatively unknown. The involvement of many other couples in the special meeting helped to disseminate the group's concerns more widely through both parishes.

The group decided to continue into a second year, studying Pope John XXIII's encyclical *Pacem in Terris,* together with documents from the Second Vatican Council. A new level of understanding and confidence was reached during this series, as members overcame remaining barriers of uncertainty and ignorance. A number of deep personal friendships were born. The new spirit within the group was one of sharing in a mutual search for answers to common questions—rather than focusing on the similarities and differences of the faiths. Again, the members became convinced that this spirit of dialogue needed wider dissemination such as had been achieved on a one-meeting basis during the first year. At the suggestion of the dialogue group, overtures were made to other Protestant churches within the general community and to individuals within our own congregations. This represented a new departure, for the first joint group had been convened entirely on the basis of personal invitation by the clergy.

A large organizational meeting was held in September. Three interfaith dialogue groups were immediately formed and so scheduled that one group would be meeting on three of the Sundays of each month. Unfortunately, members of only one other local Protestant church responded to this wider invitation. The meetings of the previous years had created such an atmosphere of trust that we dispensed with having both a Protestant pastor and a priest in attendance at each meeting of the groups. This atmosphere of trust is revealed also in the fact that a number of women from Our Lady of the Rosary parish came over to our side of the street to attend a series of lectures and discussions on the Book of Genesis during the winter and early spring. This represents to us quite a significant breakthrough: that well-educated and faithful Roman Catholic church women, several of whom held degrees from Catholic colleges, with all the lay theological sophistication that that achievement represents, should be eager to be guided in biblical interpretation by a Protestant pastor.

One of the elements which has contributed to the success of this adventure in interfaith fellowship has been the general willingness of the couples involved to abide by a series of basic ground rules that we established at an early stage. First, each participant must share, and act on, the belief that a person of the other faith is speaking in good faith. This is an indispensable minimum for any kind of dialogue. We must be able to assume a common devotion to truth. But in the Catholic-Protestant dialogue, we possess something much more significant than a common devotion to the quest for truth. We can count on a common allegiance to the One who said, "I am the way, and the truth, and the life." Catholic-Protestant discussion possesses this enormous advantage over other "interfaith" discussions: both partners share a faith in Jesus Christ. Sharing this faith makes us brethren, even though we are separated brethren.

Another ground rule is that each participant must strive for the clearest possible understanding of the other's faith. Although this understanding only emerges in full from the dialogue experience itself, it is a prerequisite in the sense that neither party has the right to waste time by starting the dialogue in total ignorance of the other's position. Both parties are required to do some serious homework in advance. A little honest reading can dispel a host of misconceptions. Related to this ground rule is another: a willingness to interpret the faith of the other party in its best light rather than its worst. Too many Protestants, when they do take the trouble to read a papal encyclical, do so simply to discover examples of what they may politely call papal dominance and less politely thought-control. They study Catholic literature simply to add fuel to their anti-Catholic fires. So, too, there are Catholics who find it difficult to take seriously the notion that anything good came out of the Reformation, or that Martin Luther was anything but an arrogant monk who could not submit to the discipline of obedience. Certainly there are many darker aspects to both Roman Catholic and Protestant traditions. Those who want to exploit them can have a field day; in fact, they can have almost anything but fruitful dialogue. One of the Protestant couples in the initial group dropped out because their anti-Catholic bias was so strong that they could not honestly agree with the spirit of this discipline. This couple was looking for debate, not dialogue, for an opportunity to score points rather than to be part of a ministry of reconciliation. A corollary to this ground rule is that each participant must maintain a continual willingness to revise his understanding of the faith of the other. Group dialogue can be a very threatening pastime, for it may force us to give up some of our most cherished caricatures of others, and these often die hard.

Furthermore, participants must forthrightly face the issues which cause separation as well as those which foster unity. If some people tend to be merely debaters, harping on the differences between Catholicism and Protestantism, there are others who in the name of a false kind of Christian charity are unwilling to confront the profound differences that do exist. Fearing that the atmosphere will be spoiled, they would like to sweep the hard issues under the rug in the name of sweet affability. This attitude is as pernicious as that of the debater. It leads to the destruction of dialogue and fellowship, for such superficial sentimentality will end in disillusionment when crucial points of division can no longer be avoided. It is far better to remind each participant at the start that mere emphasis upon points held in common will never dissipate real differences.

Finally, each participant must recognize that in the end all we can do with the dialogue is to offer it up to God. What happens in the end must be left in His hands. If something is to come of it, he will see to it. If we attempt to manipulate the dialogue we will surely thwart whatever potential good lies within it. If we are impatient for immediate results, we will simply have to learn something about the patience of God. This means, of course, that the proper atmosphere for such dialogue is above all the atmosphere of prayer, and that praying together should be part of our dialogue. If we are really willing to leave the outcome in God's hands, with all the risks that involves, this means simply that we are offering our dialogue to him in prayer, asking him to do with it as he wills, rather than as we will, and recognizing that whatever new forms of unity in thought and action may come are to be by his leading.

I believe God has already brought forth important fruits of reconciliation, unintended and unplanned by us, in his own way, out of the experience of dialogue between these two congregations. It was not our goal or expectation that participants would experience in this dialogue a deeper and more meaningful quality of Christian fellowship than they had ever known before within their own congregations; yet this unanticipated gift of grace has been attested by both Catholic and Protestant participants. We have learned through our obedience in interfaith dialogue to come to know one another, both in our similarities and in our differences, in our respective glories and in our respective shamefulness, and to offer this common endeavor to God, for him to use as he chooses.

The mandate and imperative we have for reaching out from our own parish in fellowship with other Christians goes beyond the effort to understand one another through dialogue. It is also a call to concerted action in the better fulfillment of our common mission. I am speaking now of the imperatives for developing strategies of interparish cooperation. With few exceptions, pastors and directors of Christian education are called to serve a particular congregation. It is true that they are also members of larger representative denominational bodies, with the attendant duties which involve them in service to the wider church. But essentially it is the one-man, one-church relationship which predominates. This is surely, in many ways, an efficient arrangement, but there are increasing indications in our time that it is far from adequate. Our resources as individual congregations do not match the needs of our day.

One of the most obvious evidences of our lack is visible in our educational ministry. The field of education in our generation is becoming increasingly complex. Individual ministers or directors of Christian education cannot be fully qualified to direct all the complex aspects of a full-orbed educational program adequate to the diverse needs of a modern congregation. No one person has all the specialized knowledge and skills that are needed. Yet these skills must come from somewhere, because the church cannot afford to be any less competent than secular training in its educational enterprise.

The central factor is the lay teacher himself, whether he serves in the church school, a weekday released-time program, an after-school program, or a vacation church school. This lay teacher is the key to the educational effectiveness of the church. Good curricular materials are important, good classroom facilities are helpful, audio-visual equipment can contribute, but it is the teacher who does the teaching. There is little doubt that this teacher will continue in the future to be a layman. But he should be a layman only in the sense that he is not an ordained clergyman, not in the sense of lacking expertise as a teacher. Some large congregations manage fairly effective programs of teacher training and teacher support, but most small or moderate-sized congregations do little or nothing. Is it not possible that several congregations working together could do this far more effectively?

Perhaps the most critical point is the need for high-quality adult education in the parish. The church today tries to make it clear to all its members that education in the Christian faith is a lifelong venture, that the complexities of faithful discipleship in our times call for ongoing study and training. Most church members, however, just do not take this claim seriously, one reason being that the kinds of educational programs they are said to require are not available to them. They sense that they lack a deeper understanding that will relate their faith creatively to the realities of their lives. But the minimal and traditional programs of many an individual congregation often appear irrelevant and superficial. Only a wide variety of opportunities for study on ever deeper levels of Christian maturity can meet their need. This variety and depth can seldom be provided by any one church. Cooperative planning and scheduling among several congregations, sharing of facilities and materials and, especially, leadership, hold promise of meeting a need that will become increasingly urgent in the days and years ahead.

A related area of need which demands a functional fellowship beyond the local parish is the mission of the laity in the world. Here there is an unprecedented opportunity for cooperative effort, for the world of daily work confronts the church as an ecumenical challenge. Functional and friendship relations within the occupational community have little or no correlation with denominational or parish identity. For laymen seeking to discover and test their ministry in the world, the vital common denominator is their shared concern for similar responsibilities in secular life. Special vocational concern groups, which include representatives from a number of parishes, are one of the most fruitful means for interpreting the Christian mission in the world. Furthermore, the chances for the success of such a group are high. Ecumenical discussions conducted over the years by the Department on Laity of the World Council of Churches have revealed a strong theological consensus concerning the basic nature of the ministry of the laity in the world, a consensus almost approaching unanimity when compared with discussions on other questions of faith and order. An ecumenically composed group, gathered from a number of congregations and created for the purpose of training vocationally specialized laymen for their ministry in the secular order, can assume a surprisingly wide area of essential theological agreement concerning its central aim, with little fear of treading on any denomination's doctrinal toes in having its laymen participate in the enterprise. Any purely denominational type of approach develops by its own narrow logic into the absurd and scandalous specter of Methodist dentists and Luthern machinists and Presbyterian salesmen meeting separately all around the community. What could be more foolish than such nonfunctional divisions?

The strategy that seems to be called for by these and other needs is one which provides for a variety of alignments or clusters of churches, in some cases all of one denomination, in other cases of several denominations and sometimes including Roman Catholics. We have foolishly tended to assume that the only viable lines of interparish cooperation and fellowship in mission were those of the area denominational unit, or the local council of churches, or the ministerial association or alliance. These are old forms, and in many ways they are not at all suited for the kind of strengthening through cooperative mission called for and pointed to by some of the strategic needs I have cited. The area of a denominational association is often too scattered geographically, or includes too many basically dissimilar types of congregational life (rural, inner-city, and suburban), to provide common ground for joint enterprise. Area councils of churches have the same handicaps, with such additional drawbacks as wider doctrinal differences, the apathetic disinclination of many churches toward council-sponsored program innovations, and a hardening of the institutional arteries in many conciliar structures that makes difficult the introduction of new ideas for cooperating in Christian mission. Ministerial associations may present a more geographically compact and manageable unit, but here again great diversities in doctrine and congregational style may preclude meaningful interparish ventures.

But why should we confine our thinking along these lines to the denominational area unit, the council of churches, or the ministerial alliance? Why can we not employ some imagination and create a variety of clusters of churches, specific alliances to meet specific needs? A geographically compact cluster of churches of the same denomination may be the most suitable vehicle of mission for such tasks as teacher education and church officer training, because of denominational peculiarities in church school curriculum and church officer responsibility. On the other hand, an interdenominational area cluster may be the most viable means of strengthening ministry to high school and college-age youth, or for providing church school classes for the mentally retarded, or for providing a lay school of theology or other opportunities in adult Christian education.

I would like to illustrate what I mean by reference to that with which I am most familiar. My congregation was recently involved in several different alignments of churches for different purposes of mission. We had a special alignment with the local Disciples of Christ and Methodist churches for an ecumenical youth service and weekend retreat. We were aligned with four other churches in the rental of a series of filmed lectures because the fee was greater than any one parish could afford for a moderate-sized viewing group. And, perhaps most significant of all, we created a special cluster within our denominational area unit: Within the official Presbytery of Cincinnati (which consists of seventy-eight churches and over 38,000 Presbyterians) we created a little presbytery, as it were—a cluster of five churches with a total membership of 2,000. During the past year, the six pastors of these five churches each taught one carefully prepared study course for adults two separate times. This meant that, in addition to those opportunities for adult Christian nurture which we were providing separately, there were twelve more courses—including systematic theology, the major prophets, the Gospel of Mark, ecumenical Christianity, liturgical studies, and Christian ethics—jointly offered in our cluster area. In addition, we pooled our resources for a workshop for both new and experienced teachers and for youth group advisers, and offered three special training courses. We also jointly sponsored a weekend retreat for the training of the newly elected officers of the governing boards of the five congregations. Following and paralleling the pattern of our denomination, our five-church cluster supports its activities by means of a per capita "tax" on each congregation, and elects elders in equal numbers with the clergy to a governing board which determines the cluster's policies and the scope of our joint endeavors.

I am not satisfied that this complex interweaving of alliances in mission is sufficient. I would welcome some alignments following patterns of vocational specialization, especially the gathering of vocational concern groups. I would like to see even more opportunities for adult Christian growth opened up by cooperation along interdenominational lines in addition to our denominational cluster. Yet the scope and the depth of our church's mission and ministry have been powerfully abetted by the functional alliances we have already established.

Critics of the institutional church have scored some telling hits when they have pointed to the waste of human resources, both lay and clerical, in all the minutiae of parish administration, the introverted nature of its concerns, and the lack of relevant specialization in its ministry to an increasingly specialized world. Increased dependence upon the strategy of clustering would, I believe, give adequate answer to a great many of these very valid charges being leveled at the parish church. The strategy of clustering nurtures and fosters a needed specialization of function in the form of a coordinated team of professional church workers. We need to learn to trust and rely on one another, across parish lines, as we have never done before. For far too long now we have spoken of diverse gifts of ministry, using St. Paul's analogy of the hands and arms, the varied members of the Body of Christ, as if this analogy had relevance only within the local parish. Cannot a cluster of churches also be described as the Body of Christ, a coordinated body of congregations, each with special contributions to make to the functioning of the whole? If the church is to fulfill its mission in our time, we must see that the analogy of the Body of Christ calls for recognizing and developing varieties and specializations of gifts, not only within particular congregations, but between congregations as well.

5

STRENGTHENING ON-THE-JOB WITNESS

There is a vast field of mission which lies beyond the shadow cast by the church spire, beyond the circle of the Christian's vocation represented by the institutional church, the family, and the school. My focus in this chapter is on opportunities for ministry which, for the most part, are found outside the residential area. Ministering to this nonresidential dimension of the layman's Christian calling is much more difficult. Nevertheless, it is an essential part of the mission of the church in preparing its laity for their own total witness in every area of their lives.

It is no secret that few clergymen are accustomed to convening groups of laity for the express purpose of strengthening their ministry in their daily occupations. Clergymen are understandably timid in this regard, because of their awareness of the complexity of lay people's vocational involvements in contemporary work life. It is a large and venturesome step to move from considerations of church structures and the family, where the religious professional feels reasonably familiar and competent, into what is largely a foreign territory.

I would suggest that a first step into this wider world of vocational concern might be the convening of groups of people from what may be called the helping professions or the service professions. By these terms I mean such callings as medicine, teaching, counseling, social work, and, in business and commercial life, those who are in sales or personnel work. Quite obviously, these occupational groups are likely to form a sizeable segment within many congregations. From this large minority a smaller minority of those genuinely concerned with considering together their responsibility in the light of Christian mandates could easily be gathered. There are obvious advantages to beginning with this type of group. Their common denominator is their primary relatedness to other *persons,* rather than to *things,* in their work. Because the nature of their work is so obviously a matter of direct and often tangible service or of personal relationships and communication, in contrast to primary relatedness to things in many technological occupations, these lines of work can probably be more immediately and totally perceived as Christian callings than can occupations in which the service factor and the interpersonal element are less apparent. In addition, the professional church worker who convenes this group and acts as its resource person and who may be making his first tentative venture into the nonresidential world of Christian responsibility, will feel far less out of his element in such a context than he would in meeting, say, with a group of engineers or research people. The professional church worker, by the very nature of his own training and experience, is most proficient in the area of human relations. The convening of even a considerably diversified group whose members share a Christian concern for better human relations in work life will allow him to function most effectively and to gain confidence and experience in a type of Christian encounter that may be totally new to him.

For all its vocational diversity, a group of people who work with people could address itself to such problems as these: working with highly authoritarian types of people as peers, subordinates, and superiors; acting as Christian agents of reconciliation in intergroup conflict within large educational or commercial organizations; improving communication, both upward and downward, within organizational pyramids of authority; increasing motivation and morale; and the question of how the Christian layman may be a means of grace in bringing others to give of their best in service to their fellows.

One of the most helpful resources for such a general group is *Salty Christians* by Hans-Ruedi Weber,[1] associate director of the Ecumenical Institute of the World Council of Churches and onetime executive secretary of the World Council's Department on Laity. The book is based on a handbook for lay training which Weber wrote for the East Asian Christian Conference and which he personally used in lay training courses all over the world. It includes a study guide prepared by the department of Christian education of the Episcopal Church, containing excellent questions and relevant case studies from the American scene to foster discussion. This resource is helpful in enabling such diverse persons as union shop stewards or department managers or school principals to see that the various subgroups of which they are a part at work are, as it were, little congregations within which they are called of God to exercise pastoral care as laymen, and it gives some incisive insights for this lay ministry. Another resource we found helpful in a concern group of persons from helping and service professions is Paul Tournier's book *The Meaning of Persons*.[2] We used this as a basic resource for a four-week series, supplemented with short lectures on pastoral psychology and some counseling interviews to be discussed as case studies in small groups. One of the most rewarding fruits of this vocational dialogue is the down-to-earth insight and practical guidance which emerge from the laymen's own experience and professional knowledge, as they share and discover new dimensions of what it personally means to be a means of grace to others—to be, in Luther's phrase, a Christ to one's brethren.

Even in dealing with a more technically oriented group, the religious professional's greatest contribution still will be in the dimension of Christian leavening of human relationships. In more technically specialized groups, it is helpful for the religious professional to be as knowledgeable as possible concerning new theories of commercial and industrial organization, modern economics and philosophies and styles of management, all as background to his better functioning. Yet the central task is still to foster the Christian's skills in compassion, his ways of being a personal resource to other persons. Simply to stimulate authentic human communication within the social structures of work is surely one of the most noteworthy Christian services a concern group can perform. It is a service which reaches not only its own immediate membership, but also those others with whom group members may come in contact during the course of their daily round.

Among fellow workers in any office or plant there is often a great deal of talk about matters of mutual interest related to their immediate work objectives. Usually, however, this is purely technical "shop-talk" or little more than a trading of platitudes which uncritically reflect the approved ideology of the professional, commercial, or industrial ingroup to which they all belong. In the course of their life at work people seldom have the opportunity to talk together about the basic human problems inherent in their work situations, and to discuss these situations in an atmosphere of freedom and acceptance. The church serves the world by providing arenas for such communication. Concern groups, by providing a humanizing influence upon those who directly participate and upon those who come in touch with these participants, can help to counteract the dehumanizing obstacles to communication which seem to characterize so much of modern work life. Whatever serves to make life more truly human serves the purposes of One who sent his Son as perfect man that our own humanity might be restored and redeemed through him.

The church today can be of immense redemptive value as servant in God's world by simply providing opportunities for reflective thinking and the exchange of ideas and feelings. This kind of vital conversation is too often crowded out, at home and at work, by daily crises and deadlines, and by escapist small talk which skirts enounter with life's deepest issues. In forming concern groups, the church is fostering the kind of serious two-way conversation so often lacking not only around the family table but also in the company lunchroom and in political and civic groups of various sorts. One of the most rewarding aspects of involvement in this kind of group experience is hearing, after a particular series of meetings is past, that pairs and trios of concerned laymen continue to meet on their own. They continue to deal with substantive issues of meaning in their daily work, at a level of seriousness and candor which was initiated by the structured group series. I believe that the Christian church is fulfilling a part of its intended servant role whenever it provides group training which improves the functioning of human society, whenever it helps to counteract some of the demonic distortions in interpersonal relationships which curb human creativity and personal growth. Whatever facilitates serious communication, not only among husbands and wives and neighbors, but also among superiors and subordinates and peers at work, creating an atmosphere of receptivity to criticism and to the introduction of new ideas, makes life more human and so serves God's purposes for man in the world.

Having spoken in such glowing terms of the redemptive potential in such groups, it is appropriate to suggest methods for realizing this potential. I believe there are certain basic procedures which are valid for all types of vocational concern groups regardless of the degree of specialization represented. One cardinal principle to be observed is that concern groups should talk (as the phrase itself suggests) about their real concerns, about the problems the members encounter in their particular vocational settings and just how they are experienced. One of the implications of this principle is that literature selected as material for common study needs to be treated as clearly secondary to the personal experience represented in the group.

One way to guarantee that literature will be secondary to life is to work through a nuclear group, a steering or advisory committee which examines a large body of literature from which to recommend selections and adaptations for the entire group. It would have been presumptuous of me single-handedly and unilaterally to choose reading material for a group of women meeting to explore together the meaning of their feminine role in the world. A nuclear steering group is much better suited to making such selections on behalf of their fellow members. I have conducted a number of concern groups among employees of General Electric Corporation. Nearly all have made their own selections of stimulus material through a steering committee with which I met long before the larger group was convened. Materials gathered from many sources, only some of which had been suggested by me, were carefully culled by these informal committees. Group members have also taken case studies, such as those prepared by the Detroit Industrial Mission for very different kinds of industrial settings, and have adapted these case studies to make them more immediately relevant to realities in a local plant.

Case studies have a special importance in lay training. I would like to define more specifically what I mean, and to indicate the advantages which I see accruing to their use. The "case-study method" may be defined as the presentation of actual or, at least, realistically hypothetical situations or episodes to serve as a basis for group discussion. Within such a broad definition, it is evident that case studies can be presented in a wide variety of ways. Often, in industrial study groups with which I have met, case studies have been presented in printed form, perhaps as a summary paragraph or two on the announcement or agenda sheet for the day. A case study may also be an oral report of a particular experience some member of the group has had. Again, a case report can be given quite spontaneously; as part of our in-service training program for teachers, we recently held two sessions on problems of discipline and positive teacher-pupil relationships. The entire content of these meetings consisted of specific problems and encounters which the teachers brought up spontaneously in the group situation, and which were then discussed by members of the group, and by a pediatric psychiatrist and a director of Christian education whom we had especially invited to participate.

Case studies can also be given through audio-visual means, using filmed dramas or documentaries; many television documentaries are now available as films for group use. Case studies can be set forth in the form of socio-drama, as in the case of Nora Sterling's American Theater Wing plays on problems in mental health. Role-playing is another method, more informal and often most effective.

The case-study method is especially helpful in developing a group's skill in the art of human dialogue leading to reconciliation. It subjects the group to the discipline of having to construct a line of conversation and action appropriate to a concrete situation. This situation should be one which represents a common and acknowledged obstacle to dialogue and understanding in daily life. A well-chosen case study guides the group into an active relation to that situation. This method helps to strengthen the laity as ministers of reconciliation by developing skills in imaginative and empathetic perception. It gives group participants practice in projecting themselves into the emotional and intellectual world of others, and then, perhaps, in seeing more objectively their own characteristic reactions to other persons and problems.

The whole process of education for life can be conceptualized in terms of a cycle of thought leading to words leading to deeds, the whole cycle then moving to new thoughts in retrospect, and to the repetition of the cycle on a more advanced level. Group discussion among church people, however, is often characterized by abstract, generalized thought leading to abstract, generalized words, and never issuing in any particular deeds at all because of the high level of abstraction in the discussion. Beginning with abstractions based on Scripture and doctrine, a group will often launch into an exchange of theological observations but fail to complete the cycle through some discovery of the relevance of these abstract words to concrete deeds in the daily vocational involvements of the laity. The use of the case-study method allows a group to enter this thought-word-deed cycle at its most concrete and life-centered point. It compels discussion to start with the real or at least realistically hypothetical deed represented by the case study in question. Moving from consideration of the specific case or deed, a group then can turn to the content of Christian thought, perhaps calling upon the religious professional as resource person and confronting their faith with pointed and concrete questions.

Since ethics is preeminently concerned with deeds, the case-study technique is particularly helpful in getting at the root of ethical questions in a group of concerned lay people. The introduction of a case study in one form or another often comes as a relief to a group, especially if people have been floundering for a time at a more abstract level. It provides a situation with which participants can identify, and thereby helps to restore a sense of reality to the discussion. After a case has been presented and considered, the discussion of deeper underlying issues and general ethical imperatives is made much more vital by virtue of its relation to a common base of experience. Case studies are particularly well suited to discussions centering around the ethical aspects of the layman's decision-making ministry in the paths of daily work. But the method is also helpful in opening up discussions in quite different areas, areas such as the training of laity in their pastoral function as Christian counselors and guides, through the use of psychologically oriented case studies available from counseling files. I would stress again that cases need not be factual, even in part, so long as they reflect thorough knowledge of the experiences and concerns which the members of the group hold in common. Nothing stimulates creative response more effectively than a case study which rings true; nothing falls as flat as one which sounds trumped-up. A hypothetical or heavily disguised case may be the only way of enabling a group to deal with an issue without violating confidences, indulging in scapegoating, or jeopardizing someone's job relationships. Seldom have I found myself introducing a case. This is a function, in a vast variety of discussion groups, in which the layman can and should take the lead, for he is the professional while the religious professional is the amateur.

Alan Walker, pastor of the Central Methodist Mission in Sydney, Australia, draws together each weekday noon a group called "The Crossroads Club," representing important decision-makers in the city. Walker's intention is to meet with them at the point of their special competence and concerns in the world, in their full secular integrity. The subjects under discussion in this group are the key issues emerging in the life of the city. The dialogue with the gospel to discover the concrete meaning of the lordship of Christ is thus initiated by events occurring in the metropolitan area where these men have responsibility. If there arises out of that dialogue a clear mandate for some specific Christian witness, the group can move from dialogue to appropriate forms of action.

This is the type of group that the church should seek to foster in our time, where daily life is examined in the light of Christian affirmations, rather than the other way around. In the more traditional Christian group, the raw material of secular experience is used, if at all, simply as an illustrative appendage to a course in Bible study or some other form of technical theological talk. If we let real life in the world give direction to group discourse, instead of using it didactically to illustrate some theological point, if, in other words, we allow real life to raise the questions in terms which laymen most readily understand, then we are compelled to give a disciplined response as Christians to a practical situation. The realities of the members' responsibilities in the world, with their special demands, satisfactions, problems, and pressures, pose the question, or questions, to which the Christian gospel can properly address responsible and relevant answers. It is the task of the religious professional to help laymen to structure and formulate both the questions and the answers in their own terms. To do this he must listen carefully to what laymen say about their lives and the nature of their responsibilities in the world.

Whenever a group of concerned Christians initiates conversation about a secular issue, it is not long before someone says, "This is all very interesting and important, but what in the world does it have to do with religion?" This question is sometimes voiced by new-comers to vocational concern groups when talk focuses on such worldly issues as the effects of automation, the proper role of unions, or the pros and cons of a shorter work week. How does the religious professional respond to this sincere question? By way of reply, let us suppose that a group has gathered to discuss the lively issue of how to maintain one's individuality and authentic selfhood in a large industrial or commercial organization. Typical comments heard early in the discussion may include the following: "The trouble around here is that we have too many individualists and we just can't get the job done properly." Someone else may chime in, "People think they can do things their own way." Another may add, "Wait a minute! You can't force everyone into the same mold." So it is likely to go, until more fundamental issues begin to come to the surface: "How much freedom should people have to make their own decisions on the job?" "How much of my own individuality should I be required to suppress for the good of the organization?" "Shouldn't we have the right to set our own pace?" "Is good pay the only satisfaction I should expect from my work?" Do such questions lie outside the immediate concern of Christians?

Christians have traditionally affirmed certain truths about man: he is a unique and unrepeatable person of intrinsic worth and dignity, made to receive and give companionship, who needs to be a part of some significant group, who has the capacity to choose freely between various alternatives, and who has been charged with the responsibility of performing worthwhile tasks for the good of the human community. There is a vital link between these convictions and secular issues. It is found at the point where a secular issue, discussed in secular terms, reveals itself at its deeper levels as the same kind of issue to which the Christian faith has always addressed itself: what should people expect out of life and work, what is the right thing to do, what should be the quality, direction, and purpose of our existence, individually and together? To be sure, such discussions do not usually have to do with "religion" in any narrow sense of piety, worship, or interior spirituality. But secular issues contain questions of vast significance for the quality and meaning of the human scene, which has always been the terrain of Christian concern. The relationship between the individual and his work organization is just one example of a question revealing the common ground between secular problems and Christian discipleship.

A group discussion can be profoundly theological whenever it deals with ultimate questions raised by the "worldly" concerns occupying the group's attention. For what is theological reflection? I think it can be fairly defined as the opening up of some of the data of our human experience to an examination of its deeper dimensions of meaning, and a consideration of who we are in terms of our present expectations, our future goals and plans, and our ultimate commitments. Such reflection can be carried on without any self-conscious dependence upon traditional theological terminology. Such a group is truly involved in the significant theological enterprise of seeking to discern the workings of God, and man's appropriate response to God's activity. An unashamedly secular orientation in group dialogue allows real life in God's world to pose its own authentic questions in its own way and in its own terms. Only then will our theological affirmations speak with both honesty and clarity to those concerns. This does not mean, by the way, that the religious professional needs to wait passively for the right questions to be asked. It is often his function to precipitate the asking of these questions, priming the group with some of his own which spring from his personal theological commitment.

The following are just a few of many basic questions to be faced by Christians in their daily work. First, how do we determine the value of a person? Within effective industrial organizations, the main test of a person is his achievement and performance on the job, his contribution to the goals of the company. Obviously this pragmatic value system of industry, and, indeed, of American society, is valuable to the degree that it unceasingly subjects programs, policies, and ideas to the test of practicality and hard results. Nevertheless, we as Christians must ask where this emphasis upon achievement is leading modern man. Is achievement the real measure of a man? Performance ratings assume some standards against which results are measured; but can an individual, in all the complexity of his talents, his potentialities, his virtues, and his failings, be accurately measured by some general yardstick? Can we ever measure the ultimate worth of a man?

Another significant general question is related to the conscientious fulfillment of one's calling in daily work: Do most administrators really understand the human need of their subordinates to have some share in the decisions which affect them? At all levels in industry and commerce, participative decision-making certainly lags far behind the democratic political assumptions which most Americans hold. There are exceptional organizations where a broad base of people formulate many major decisions, but they are proportionately few. The time is certainly ripe for more intensive implementation of the expanding social and psychological knowledge about what motivates people and what makes organizations tick. Few executives today would hold that no one should do more than carry out orders. The question is not whether participative management should be developed and enlarged, but how.

A third basic question has to do with ethics. It is obvious that many of the most effective business and professional men approach moral decisions situationally. In response to the question of how rules and principles are applied to concrete situations, their usual reply is, "It all depends." The ethics of many people in their work life are fairly pragmatic. This is surely commendable in part, for it focuses upon the moral consequences of any decision that is made. But purely pragmatic decision-making poses serious challenges to Christian ethical norms. This kind of decision-making makes it imperative for us to relate our value system to results, which is infinitely more complex than relating values to motives and intentions alone. People need to face such questions as these: Can we always predict consequences with sufficient accuracy so that we do not have to fall back on tested moral principles? How can we be sure that we always consider all of the consequences? How can we be sure that we have given balanced and objective consideration to all those involved in the consequences? Does not a persistent attention simply to results make a person insensitive to the limits beyond which he should not go to achieve a good end?

Such questions, posed in secular language, call for theological response. The role of theology is to provide a comprehensive view of the meaning of life, as well as a perspective from which to judge situations, to set priorities, and to weigh alternatives. In this way, theology provides a background for concrete decisions by the Christian worker. Vocational concern groups can also express Christian social responsibility. The Christian gospel properly should serve individuals *and* their organizations in such a way as to help both to be effective and responsible. We have a ministry not only to individuals as such but also to the structures within which the lives of individuals are shaped. Vocational concern groups centered beyond the residential base constitute an effective means of helping to transform secular structures into greater conformity with the mandates of the Christian gospel.

POSTSCRIPT

There has been a centrifugal progression in these brief chapters, an outward movement from the sanctuary and classrooms of the local church into the home, the school, the neighboring community, other churches, and even company lunchrooms and board rooms. This progression reflects a belief that "reviving the local church" is impossible if we concentrate on its internal operations, that to seek the church's life this way is to lose it. I do not mean to imply, of course, that we should ever neglect the vital center of public worship and parish education as we seek relevant involvement in the life of our times; too many Christian movements into the world have gone spiritually bankrupt by forgetting their ultimate reason and transcendent motive for being there. Nevertheless, our mandate for mission is a call to turn the ecclesiastical institution from itself outward to the world and its needs.

To be the local "church-in-mission" to the world is first of all to be a *communicating* church. The strategies and experiments explored in the foregoing chapters are efforts to open and deepen the channels of communication. We have much to learn about the secular forms of thought, speech, and activity that dominate the lives of men today. We have translated the Bible into thousands of languages and dialects, but we have not kept up with the task of translating biblical concepts into the *lingua franca* of our times. We need to engage in "gossiping the gospel," in D. T. Niles' phrase, using an increasingly secular language and less "God-talk" in modern Christian discourse.

A major function of the kinds of dialogue I have mentioned is to achieve such translation. To the extent that dialogue attains this goal, the transforming power of the gospel can move along opened channels to change thoughts and attitudes and actions. Many critics both within and outside the church scoff at the church educator's preoccupation with problems of communication, saying they want less talk and more action. I believe these critics fail to perceive how much social as well as personal change is the result of effective communication leading to new experience and understanding. They are inclined to overlook or discount the demonstrable shifts of attitude among church people in recent years which have provided the necessary base for new departures in social and ecumenical action, as well as new forms of ministry. I am convinced that the life of intensive dialogue, to the extent that it is biblically informed, will drive us from reflection to action, from internalized preoccupation with the institutional church and its people outward toward all the institutions and people of God's world.

NOTES

1. *To Be Is to Teach*

1. John W. Meister, quoted in *The Church and Its Changing Ministry,* ed. Robert Clyde Johnson (Philadelphia: General Assembly, 1961), p. 176.

2. Quotations from "The Confession of 1967," in *The Book of Confessions* (Philadelphia: General Assembly, 1967).

3. George F. MacLeod, *"We Shall Rebuild"* (Glasgow: Iona Community, 1947), p. 66.

4. Reuel L. Howe, *Man's Need and God's Action* (Greenwich: Seabury, 1953), p. 46.

5. Lewis J. Sherrill, *The Gift of Power* (New York: Macmillan, 1955), p. 82.

6. John Calvin, *The Institutes of the Christian Religion* (London: James Clarke, 1953), Vol. IV, chap. i.5, p. 284.

7. Richard Baxter, *The Reformed Pastor* (Hudson, Ohio: Sawyer, Ingersoll & Co., 1852), p. 24.

8. Donald W. Crawford, *A Parish Workshop in Christian Education* (Greenwich: Seabury, 1953).

9. Hendrik Kraemer, *The Communication of the Christian Faith* (Philadelphia: Westminster, 1956), p. 27.

2. *Preaching for Renewal*

1. Wilhelm Pauck, "The Ministry in the Time of the Continental Reformation," *The Ministry in Historical Perspectives* (New York: Harper, 1956), p. 135.

Notes

2. Reuel L. Howe, "The Recovery of Dialogue in Preaching," *Pastoral Psychology,* XII (October, 1961), 14.

3. A fuller description may be found in Browne Barr's *Parish Back Talk* (Nashville: Abingdon Press, 1964).

4. The experience of this congregation has been reported in a mimeographed address given by the pastor, the Rev. Harold H. Byers, Jr., of the Presbyterian Church of the Apostles, to a 1967 meeting of the Presbyterian Board of National Missions.

5. "Westminster Larger Catechism," *The Constitution of the United Presbyterian Church in the USA* (Philadelphia: General Assembly, 1963), p. 73.

3. Service Within the Steeple's Shadow

1. St. Louis: Bethany Press, 1962.

2. New York: Association Press, 1961.

3. Philadelphia: Westminster Press, 1960.

4. Philadelphia: Westminster Press, 1967.

5. Gibson Winter, *Love and Conflict: New Patterns in Family Life* (New York: Doubleday, 1958).

6. *Harper's Magazine,* CCXXX (October, 1960). Among the other works utilized by the resource group were: Richard E. Gordon, Katherine K. Gordon, and Max Gunther, *The Split-Level Trap* (New York: Dell, 1962); Betty Friedan, *The Feminine Mystique* (New York: W. W. Norton, 1963); Simone De Beauvoir, *The Second Sex* (New York: Bantam, 1968); and Margaret Mead, *Male and Female* (New York: Mentor, 1960).

5. Strengthening On-the-Job Witness

1. Greenwich: Seabury Press, 1963.

2. New York: Harper & Row, 1957.

FOR FURTHER READING

BARR, BROWNE. *Parish Back Talk.* Nashville: Abingdon Press, 1964. A pastor and professor of practical theology answers critics of conventional or traditional parish structures with both practical and theological evidence rather than shrill rhetoric.

ERNSBERGER, DAVID J. *Education for Renewal.* Philadelphia: The Westminster Press, 1965. Gives further details concerning specific resources, methods, and experiments with various vocational groups.

HOWE, REUEL L. *Partners in Preaching.* New York: The Seabury Press, 1967. A theology of dialogue empirically applied to the complementary callings of clergy and laity in preaching.

GREENSPUN, WILLIAM B., and NORGREN, WILLIAM A. (eds.). *Living Room Dialogues.* New York: The National Council of Churches of Christ in the U. S. A., 1965. Jointly published by the National Council of Churches and the Paulist Fathers, this paperback is designed to provide resources for seven sessions of ecumenical conversation, but we have found here stimulation for many more than that.

RAINES, ROBERT A. *New Life in the Church.* New York: Harper and Row, 1961. Similar to Barr's book in that it gives glimpses from another parish situation of what the church can be and do.